**Great Works** Instructional G for **Literature**

Out of My Mind

A guide for the novel by Sharon M. Draper
Great Works Author: Suzanne Barchers

 **SHELL EDUCATION**

Publishing Credits

Corinne Burton, M.A.Ed., *President*; Conni Medina, M.A.Ed., *Managing Editor*; Emily R. Smith, M.A.Ed., *Content Director*; Lee Aucoin, *Senior Graphic Designer*; Charles Feinson, *Editor*; Stephanie Bernard, *Assistant Editor*; Don Tran, *Graphic Designer*

Image Credits

iStock (cover)

Standards

© 2007 Teachers of English to Speakers of Other Languages, Inc. (TESOL)
© 2007 Board of Regents of the University of Wisconsin System. World-Class Instructional Design and Assessment (WIDA)
© Copyright 2010. National Governors Association Center for Best Practices and Council of Chief State School Officers. All rights reserved.
© Copyright 2007–2015. Texas Education Association (TEA). All rights reserved.

Shell Education

A division of Teacher Created Materials
5301 Oceanus Drive
Huntington Beach, CA 92649-1030
ISBN 978-1-4807-8511-3
https://www.tcmpub.com/shell-education
© 2017 Shell Educational Publishing, Inc.

The classroom teacher may reproduce copies of materials in this book for classroom use only. The reproduction of any part for an entire school or school system is strictly prohibited. No part of this publication may be transmitted, stored, or recorded in any form without written permission from the publisher.

Table of Contents

How to Use This Literature Guide

Today's standards demand rigor and relevance in the reading of complex texts. The units in this series guide teachers in a rich and deep exploration of worthwhile works of literature for classroom study. The most rigorous instruction can also be interesting and engaging!

Many current strategies for effective literacy instruction have been incorporated into these instructional guides for literature. Throughout the units, text-dependent questions are used to determine comprehension of the book as well as student interpretation of the vocabulary words. The books chosen for the series are complex exemplars of carefully crafted works of literature. Close reading is used throughout the units to guide students toward revisiting the text and using textual evidence to respond to prompts orally and in writing. Students must analyze the story elements in multiple assignments for each section of the book. All of these strategies work together to rigorously guide students through their study of literature.

The next few pages will make clear how to use this guide for a purposeful and meaningful literature study. Each section of this guide is set up in the same way to make it easier for you to implement the instruction in your classroom.

Theme Thoughts

The great works of literature used throughout this series have important themes that have been relevant to people for many years. Many of the themes will be discussed during the various sections of this instructional guide. However, it would also benefit students to have independent time to think about the key themes of the novel.

Before students begin reading, have them complete *Pre-Reading Theme Thoughts* (page 13). This graphic organizer will allow students to think about the themes outside the context of the story. They'll have the opportunity to evaluate statements based on important themes and defend their opinions. Be sure to have students keep their papers for comparison to the *Post-Reading Theme Thoughts* (page 64). This graphic organizer is similar to the pre-reading activity. However, this time, students will be answering the questions from the point of view of one of the characters in the novel. They have to think about how the character would feel about each statement and defend their thoughts. To conclude the activity, have students compare what they thought about the themes before they read the novel to what the characters discovered during the story.

How to Use This Literature Guide (cont.)

Vocabulary

Each teacher overview page has definitions and sentences about how key vocabulary words are used in the section. These words should be introduced and discussed with students. There are two student vocabulary activity pages in each section. On the first page, students are asked to define the ten words chosen by the author of this unit. On the second page in most sections, each student will select at least eight words that he or she finds interesting or difficult. For each section, choose one of these pages for your students to complete. With either assignment, you may want to have students get into pairs to discuss the meanings of the words. Allow students to use reference guides to define the words. Monitor students to make sure the definitions they have found are accurate and relate to how the words are used in the text.

On some of the vocabulary student pages, students are asked to answer text-related questions about the vocabulary words. The following question stems will help you create your own vocabulary questions if you'd like to extend the discussion.

- How does this word describe _____'s character?
- In what ways does this word relate to the problem in this story?
- How does this word help you understand the setting?
- In what ways is this word related to the story's solution?
- Describe how this word supports the novel's theme of . . . .
- What visual images does this word bring to your mind?
- For what reasons might the author have chosen to use this particular word?

At times, more work with the words will help students understand their meanings. The following quick vocabulary activities are a good way to further study the words.

- Have students practice their vocabulary and writing skills by creating sentences and/or paragraphs in which multiple vocabulary words are used correctly and with evidence of understanding.
- Students can play vocabulary concentration. Students make a set of cards with the words and a separate set of cards with the definitions. Then, students lay the cards out on the table and play concentration. The goal of the game is to match vocabulary words with their definitions.
- Students can create word journal entries about the words. Students choose words they think are important and then describe why they think each word is important within the novel.

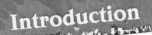

How to Use This Literature Guide *(cont.)*

Analyzing the Literature

After students have read each section, hold small-group or whole-class discussions. Questions are written at two levels of complexity to allow you to decide which questions best meet the needs of your students. The Level 1 questions are typically less abstract than the Level 2 questions. Level 1 is indicated by a square, while Level 2 is indicated by a triangle. These questions focus on the various story elements, such as character, setting, and plot. Student pages are provided if you want to assign these questions for individual student work before your group discussion. Be sure to add further questions as your students discuss what they've read. For each question, a few key points are provided for your reference as you discuss the novel with students.

Reader Response

In today's classrooms, there are often great readers who are below-average writers. So much time and energy is spent in classrooms getting students to read on grade level that little time is left to focus on writing skills. To help teachers include more writing in their daily literacy instruction, each section of this guide has a literature-based reader response prompt. Each of the three genres of writing is used in the reader responses within this guide: narrative, informative/explanatory, and opinion/argument. Students have a choice between two prompts for each reader response. One response requires students to make connections between the reading and their own lives. The other prompt requires students to determine text-to-text connections or connections within the text.

Close Reading the Literature

Within each section, students are asked to closely reread a short section of text. Since some versions of the novels have different page numbers, the selections are described by chapter and location, along with quotations to guide the readers. After each close reading, there are text-dependent questions to be answered by students.

Encourage students to read each question one at a time and then go back to the text and discover the answer. Work with students to ensure that they use the text to determine their answers rather than making unsupported inferences. Once students have answered the questions, discuss what they discovered. Suggested answers are provided in the answer key.

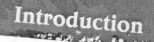

How to Use This Literature Guide (cont.)

Close Reading the Literature (cont.)

The generic, open-ended stems below can be used to write your own text-dependent questions if you would like to give students more practice.

- Give evidence from the text to support . . . .
- Justify your thinking using text evidence about . . . .
- Find evidence to support your conclusions about . . . .
- What text evidence helps the reader understand . . . ?
- Use the book to tell why _____ happens.
- Based on events in the story, ...
- Use text evidence to describe why . . . .

Making Connections

The activities in this section help students make cross-curricular connections to writing, mathematics, science, social studies, or the fine arts. Each of these types of activities requires higher-order thinking skills from students.

Creating with the Story Elements

It is important to spend time discussing the common story elements in literature. Understanding the characters, setting, and plot can increase students' comprehension and appreciation of the story. If teachers discuss these elements daily, students will more likely internalize the concepts and look for the elements in their independent reading. Another important reason for focusing on the story elements is that students will be better writers if they think about how the stories they read are constructed.

Students are given three options for working with the story elements. They are asked to create something related to the characters, setting, or plot of the novel. Students are given a choice in this activity so that they can decide to complete the activity that most appeals to them. Different multiple intelligences are used so that the activities are diverse and interesting to all students.

How to Use This Literature Guide (cont.)

Culminating Activity

This open-ended, cross-curricular activity requires higher-order thinking and allows for a creative product. Students will enjoy getting the chance to share what they have discovered through reading the novel. Be sure to allow them enough time to complete the activity at school or home.

Comprehension Assessment

The questions in this section are modeled after current standardized tests to help students analyze what they've read and prepare for tests they may see in their classrooms. The questions are dependent on the text and require critical-thinking skills to answer.

Response to Literature

The final post-reading activity is an essay based on the text that also requires further research by students. This is a great way to extend this book into other curricular areas. A suggested rubric is provided for teacher reference.

Correlation to the Standards

Shell Education is committed to producing educational materials that are research and standards based. As part of this effort, we have correlated all of our products to the academic standards of all 50 states, the District of Columbia, the Department of Defense Dependents Schools, and all Canadian provinces.

Purpose and Intent of Standards

The Every Student Succeeds Act (ESSA) mandates that all states adopt challenging academic standards that help students meet the goal of college and career readiness. While many states already adopted academic standards prior to ESSA, the act continues to hold states accountable for detailed and comprehensive standards. Standards are statements that describe the criteria necessary for students to meet specific academic goals. They define the knowledge, skills, and content students should acquire at each level. State standards are used in the development of our products, so educators can be assured they meet state academic requirements.

How to Find Standards Correlations

To print a customized correlation report of this product for your state, visit our website at **www.teachercreatedmaterials.com/administrators/correlations/** and follow the online directions. If you require assistance in printing correlation reports, please contact our Customer Service Department at 1-877-777-3450.

Correlation to the Standards (cont.)

Standards Correlation Chart

The lessons in this guide were written to support today's college and career readiness standards. This chart indicates which sections of this guide address which standards.

College and Career Readiness Standard	Section
Read closely to determine what the text says explicitly and to make logical inferences from it; cite specific textual evidence when writing or speaking to support conclusions drawn from the text.	Close Reading the Literature Sections 1–5
Determine central ideas or themes of a text and analyze their development; summarize the key supporting details and ideas.	Analyzing the Literature Sections 1–5; Reader Response Sections 1–5; Making Connections Sections 1, 3–5; Creating with Story Elements Sections 1, 3, 5; Response to Literature
Analyze how and why individuals, events, or ideas develop and interact over the course of a text.	Analyzing the Literature Sections 1–5; Reader Response Sections 1–5; Creating with Story Elements Sections 1–5
Interpret words and phrases as they are used in a text, including determining technical, connotative, and figurative meanings, and analyze how specific word choices shape meaning or tone.	Vocabulary Sections 1–5; Close Reading the Literature Sections 1–5
Analyze the structure of texts, including how specific sentences, paragraphs, and larger portions of the text (e.g., a section, chapter, scene, or stanza) relate to each other and the whole.	Analyzing the Literature Sections 1–5; Creating with Story Elements Sections 1–5
Assess how point of view or purpose shapes the content and style of a text.	Analyzing the Literature Sections 1–5; Reader Response Sections 1–5
Write arguments to support claims in an analysis of substantive topics or texts using valid reasoning and relevant and sufficient evidence.	Reader Response Sections 1–5; Response to Literature; Making Connections Section 2
Write informative/explanatory texts to examine and convey complex ideas and information clearly and accurately through the effective selection, organization, and analysis of content.	Reader Response Sections 1–5
Write narratives to develop real or imagined experiences or events using effective technique, well-chosen details and well-structured event sequences.	Reader Response Sections 1–5
Produce clear and coherent writing in which the development, organization, and style are appropriate to task, purpose, and audience.	Reader Response Sections 1–5; Making Connections Section 2; Culminating Activity; Response to Literature
Use technology, including the Internet, to produce and publish writing and to interact and collaborate with others.	Making Connections Section 3
Conduct short as well as more sustained research projects based on focused questions, demonstrating understanding of the subject under investigation.	Making Connections Section 3

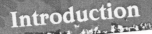

Correlation to the Standards (cont.)

Standards Correlation Chart (cont.)

College and Career Readiness Standard	Section
Draw evidence from literary or informational texts to support analysis, reflection, and research.	Reader Response Sections 1–5; Response to Literature
Write routinely over extended time frames (time for research, reflection, and revision) and shorter time frames (a single sitting or a day or two) for a range of tasks, purposes, and audiences.	Reader Response Sections 1–5; Creating with Story Elements Sections 3–5; Culminating Activity; Response to Literature
Demonstrate command of the conventions of standard English grammar and usage when writing or speaking.	Reader Response Sections 1–5; Making Connections Section 2; Creating with Story Elements Sections 3–5; Culminating Activity; Response to Literature
Demonstrate command of the conventions of standard English capitalization, punctuation, and spelling when writing.	Reader Response Sections 1–5; Making Connections Section 2; Creating with Story Elements Sections 2–5; Culminating Activity; Response to Literature
Apply knowledge of language to understand how language functions in different contexts, to make effective choices for meaning or style, and to comprehend more fully when reading or listening.	Reader Response Sections 1–5; Creating with Story Elements Section 2; Culminating Activity; Response to Literature
Determine or clarify the meaning of unknown and multiple-meaning words and phrases by using context clues, analyzing meaningful word parts, and consulting general and specialized reference materials, as appropriate.	Vocabulary Sections 1–5
Demonstrate understanding of figurative language, word relationships, and nuances in word meanings.	Vocabulary Sections 1–5; Culminating Activity
Acquire and use accurately a range of general academic and domain-specific words and phrases sufficient for reading, writing, speaking, and listening at the college and career readiness level; demonstrate independence in gathering vocabulary knowledge when encountering an unknown term important to comprehension or expression.	Vocabulary Sections 1–5

TESOL and WIDA Standards

The lessons in this book promote English language development for English language learners. The following TESOL and WIDA English Language Development Standards are addressed through the activities in this book:

- Standard 1: English language learners communicate for social and instructional purposes within the school setting.

- Standard 2: English language learners communicate information, ideas and concepts necessary for academic success in the content area of language arts.

About the Author—Sharon M. Draper

Sharon Mills Draper was born August 21, 1948, in Cleveland, Ohio. Her father was a hotel manager, and her mother worked at the Cleveland Plain Dealer. Draper became an avid reader. Her parents valued education and expected that she and her siblings would attend college. As a National Merit Scholar, she completed her bachelor's degree in English at Pepperdine University. She married Larry E. Draper, an educator, and began teaching and raising her family in Cincinnati, Ohio.

Draper tackled her first major writing challenge thanks to a student who handed her an application for a writing contest. *Ebony* magazine selected her short story from among 20,000 entries as the winner. From that day forward, Draper built on this initial success, developing a remarkable career in both education and writing. Her first novel, *Tears of a Tiger,* won numerous awards, including the Coretta Scott King Genesis Award.

Draper continued to challenge and inspire her students while she wrote several notable books for teens. High school seniors who took her class had to write research papers that were considered so demanding that survivors proudly wore T-shirts proclaiming "I Survived the Draper Paper." In 1997, she was honored as the National Teacher of the Year. She became a spokesperson for education, serving as a tireless advocate for dedicated educators.

Out of My Mind was on the New York Times Best Sellers list for over 18 months and has won numerous awards. Draper turned to historical fiction when writing *Copper Sun,* a gripping novel about the slave trade in early America. Intended for young adult readers, *Copper Sun* has been chosen by the International Reading Association, the United States Department of State, and Reading Across Continents as a novel to be read by students in the United States and Africa.

Draper continues to live in Cincinnati, Ohio. She visits schools, speaks internationally, and draws upon her teaching experience to write authentic, complex young adult novels and entertaining juvenile fiction.

Possible Texts for Text Comparisons

Double Dutch explores the challenge faced by a bright, athletic young girl—being unable to read. Della is good enough to win competitions for Double Dutch jump roping. Her secret, and that of her friend Randy, provides a gripping story of how two brave eighth graders face life. Sharon Draper writes many outstanding books for teen readers, such as those in the Jericho Trilogy and the Hazelwood Trilogy.

Book Summary of *Out of My Mind*

The narrator begins the story by describing the joy she finds in words—words that have swirled around her—as "each one is delicate and different." This celebration of words ends when she shares that she is almost eleven years old and has never spoken a word.

Born with cerebral palsy, Melody needs help with every aspect of her life, from eating to dressing to using the bathroom. She recounts the challenges she faces, dating from her earliest memories. Her parents resist the notion of "warehousing" her, and they fill her life with frank conversations, encouragement, love, and humor. Melody essentially has a photographic memory, soaking in information from television programs, documentaries, audiobooks, and movies. Her brain is busy sorting and thinking about all she absorbs, but she cannot express herself.

After being enrolled in the local elementary school, Melody discovers that much of her learning depends on how astute the teacher is. While most of her teachers do relatively little harm, they do not see Melody's true abilities. However, one rare teacher recognizes that Melody can learn and think and provides her with audiobooks.

Everything begins to change the year that Melody enters fifth grade. She gets an aid to help her. She goes to inclusion classes. A girl is friendly to her, in spite of some snarky peers. And Melody discovers that there are assistive devices that can allow her to use her thumbs to communicate. At last, she can demonstrate just how bright she is.

Melody stuns the fifth grade class when she decides to try out for a place on the Whiz Kids team. Thanks to the unfailing support and coaching from her neighbor, Mrs. V, Melody attains the first perfect test score in the school's history of the contest. Although not all the team members welcome Melody, they recognize her contributions as they progress toward competing at the national level in Washington, D.C.

When Melody is packed and ready for the excitement of the trip and the competition, she is left behind. Her disappointment with her teammates plus her frustration with her physical limitations are heightened by a near-tragedy at home. Yet Melody's dignity and resolve touch all readers fortunate to meet her.

Cross-Curricular Connection

This book is ideal for a unit on empathy, facing challenges, or dealing with differences. This book can also be used during a study of human development, focusing on physical limitations and the use of assistive devices.

Possible Texts for Text Sets

- Buyea, Rob. 2011. *Because of Mr. Terupt*. New York: Yearling.
- ———. 2013. *Mr. Terupt Falls Again*. New York: Yearling.
- Palacio, R. J. 2012. *Wonder*. New York: Knopf Books for Young Readers.
- Sloan, Holly Goldberg. 2014. *Counting by 7s*. New York: Dell.

Name _____

Date _____

Pre-Reading Theme Thoughts

Directions: Read each of the statements in the first column. Decide if you agree or disagree with the statements. Record your opinion by marking an *X* in Agree or Disagree for each statement. Explain your choices in the fourth column. There are no right or wrong answers.

Statement	Agree	Disagree	Explain Your Answer
A person who can't talk probably isn't very smart.			
People who have learning disabilities should attend special classes, so they don't slow down the rest of the students.			
A person who has a hard time with a school subject just needs to study harder.			
All students should take tests in the same way so that it's fair for everyone.			

Teacher Plans

Vocabulary Overview

Ten key words from this section are provided below with definitions and sentences about how the words are used in the book. Choose one of the vocabulary activity sheets (pages 15 or 16) for students to complete as they read this section. Monitor students as they work to ensure the definitions they have found are accurate and relate to the text. Finally, discuss these important vocabulary words with students. If you think these words or other words in the section warrant more time devoted to them, there are suggestions in the introduction for other vocabulary activities (page 5).

Word	Definition	Sentence about Text
flailing (ch. 2)	thrashing; lashing out	Melody occasionally **flails** her arms.
evaluation (ch. 4)	a report that tells the value or quality of something	The doctor quickly writes up his **evaluation** of Melody.
opinions (ch. 5)	thoughts; attitudes	Carl doesn't hesitate to let everyone know what his **opinions** are.
sheepish (ch. 6)	embarrassed; awkward	Melody's dad looks **sheepish** when Mrs. V explains that she's happy to help Melody even if the pay isn't much.
glitches (ch. 6)	small problems; hitches	Melody's thumbs work without any **glitches**, just like magic.
letdown (ch. 7)	disappointment; feeling of sadness	Melody's dreams are great because she can do anything. Waking up is a **letdown**.
unraveled (ch. 7)	fell apart; became undone	One school year is awesome for Melody, but everything **unravels** with the next teacher.
spazzed (ch. 7)	acted like a klutz; acted goofy	When frustration builds up a lot, Melody reacts and gets **spazzed** out.
tersely (ch. 7)	briefly; concisely	The principal speaks **tersely** to the teacher, telling her to call Melody's mother.
exaggerating (ch. 7)	overstating; inflating	Melody's teacher thinks Melody's mom is **exaggerating** when she talks about her daughter.

© *Shell Education*

Name _____

Date _____

Understanding Vocabulary Words

Directions: The following words appear in this section of the book. Use context clues and reference materials to determine an accurate definition for each word.

Word	Definition
flailing (ch. 2)	
evaluation (ch. 4)	
opinions (ch. 5)	
sheepish (ch. 6)	
glitches (ch. 6)	
letdown (ch. 7)	
unraveled (ch. 7)	
spazzed (ch. 7)	
tersely (ch. 7)	
exaggerating (ch. 7)	

Name _____

Date _____

During-Reading Vocabulary Activity

Directions: As you read these chapters, record at least eight important words on the lines below. Try to find interesting, difficult, intriguing, special, or funny words. Your words can be long or short. They can be hard or easy to spell. After each word, use context clues in the text and reference materials to define the word.

- _____
- _____
- _____
- _____
- _____
- _____
- _____
- _____
- _____
- _____

Directions: Respond to these questions about the words in this section.

1. Use examples from the text to describe Dr. Hugely's **evaluation** of Melody.

   _____

   _____

2. Explain why Mrs. Billups thinks that Melody's mother was **exaggerating** during their last parent conference.

   _____

   _____

     © Shell Education

Analyzing the Literature

Provided below are discussion questions you can use in small groups, with the whole class, or for written assignments. Each question is given at two levels so you can choose the right question for each group of students. Activity sheets with these questions are provided (pages 18–19) if you want students to write their responses. For each question, a few key discussion points are provided for your reference.

Story Element	■ Level 1	▲ Level 2	Key Discussion Points
Character	What do you learn about the narrator of the story in chapter 1?	What important things do you learn about Melody's character in chapter 1?	The narrator, Melody, loves words. She has a good memory and has parents who talk and sing to her. Discuss how the author builds this information and then ends the chapter with the startling information that Melody has never spoken.
Plot	What decision does Melody's mom make after their visit to Dr. Hugely?	Would Melody be better off in a special facility than a public school? Why or why not?	Melody's parents send her to a public school. There are advantages and disadvantages to the school. The teachers aren't always the best. But Melody does learn from one teacher. She also gets to observe kids—but does not get to fully participate.
Character	What role does Mrs. V play in Melody's life? How does she push her?	In chapter 6, do you think Mrs. V did the right thing by making Melody roll over? Why or why not?	Mrs. V makes Melody do things. She suspects that Melody is smart and confirms that. She also gives her treats that her parents won't give her, such as soda. It may have been hopeless to make her roll over, but Melody has an important victory and shows determination.
Setting	In chapter 6, how does Melody's dad change their home to adjust it for Melody?	How does having a person in a wheelchair affect a family and its home?	Melody's dad adds a ramp to the house. The doorways must be wide enough for a wheelchair, and ramps may be needed for stairs. The family has to work together to help Melody. Melody has to be lifted in and out of bed, onto the toilet, etc.

Name _____

Date _____

Analyzing the Literature

Directions: Think about the section you just read. Read each question, and state your response with textual evidence.

1. What do you learn about the narrator of the story in chapter 1?

_____

_____

_____

_____

2. What decision does Melody's mom make after their visit to Dr. Hugely?

_____

_____

_____

_____

3. What role does Mrs. V play in Melody's life? How does she push her?

_____

_____

_____

_____

4. In chapter 6, how does Melody's dad change their home to adjust it for Melody?

_____

_____

_____

_____

Name _____

Date _____

▲ Analyzing the Literature

Directions: Think about the section you just read. Read each question, and state your response with textual evidence.

1. What important things do you learn about Melody's character in chapter 1?

   _____

   _____

   _____

   _____

2. Would Melody be better off in a special facility than a public school? Why or why not?

   _____

   _____

   _____

   _____

3. In chapter 6, do you think Mrs. V did the right thing by making Melody roll over? Why or why not?

   _____

   _____

   _____

   _____

4. How does having a person in a wheelchair affect a family and its home?

   _____

   _____

   _____

Name _____

Date _____

Reader Response

Directions: Choose one of the following prompts about this section to answer. Be sure you include a topic sentence in your response, use textual evidence to support your opinion, and provide a strong conclusion that summarizes your opinion.

Writing Prompts

- **Opinion/Argument Piece**—If you were Melody, how would you want to be cared for? Would you want to be in a place where specialized people take care of you and live away from your family? Or would you want to go to public school and live at home? Explain your choice and the benefits.
- **Informative/Explanatory Piece**—Explain how Melody's mother serves as an advocate for her when dealing with other adults. Find at least two examples, and describe how she demonstrates her belief in Melody.

_____

_____

_____

_____

_____

_____

_____

_____

_____

_____

_____

Name _____

Date _____

Close Reading the Literature

Directions: Closely reread the first seven paragraphs of chapter 7. Begin with, "When I sleep, I dream." Stop with, "It was awesome." Read each question, and then revisit the text to find evidence that supports your answer.

1. Use examples from the text that describe Melody's behavior in dreams. Contrast those acts with her feeling upon waking up.

   _____

   _____

   _____

2. What does Melody think about the classroom aides? Describe specific things the aides do.

   _____

   _____

   _____

3. Using examples from the story, explain why Mrs. Tracy's teaching is a turning point for Melody.

   _____

   _____

   _____

   _____

4. Use the text to summarize why the year with Mrs. Tracy is "awesome" for Melody.

   _____

   _____

   _____

Name _____

Date _____

Making Connections–Circles of Support

Directions: Melody is the focus of the novel. But there are other characters that provide support for her. Choose four characters from the story. Write their names in each of the circles, and briefly describe how they support Melody.

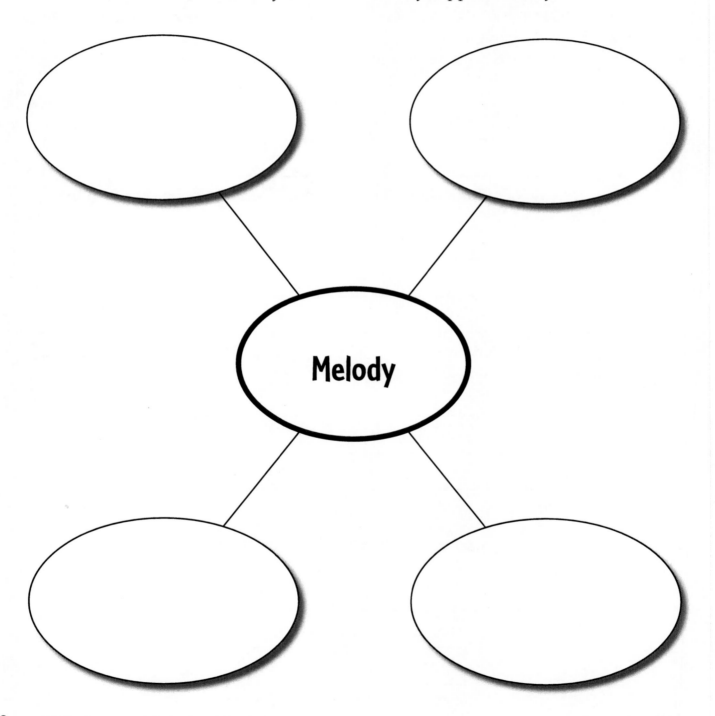

    © *Shell Education*

Name _____

Date _____

Creating with the Story Elements

Directions: Thinking about the story elements of character, setting, and plot in a novel is very important to understanding what is happening and why. Complete **one** of the following activities based on what you've read so far. Be creative, and have fun!

Characters

Create a wanted poster for Mrs. Billups. Include her characteristics, her misdeeds, and a drawing of how you think she looks.

Setting

Create a model of the classroom snowman described in chapter 5. Use any medium you'd like, and include details of how it's dressed, its appearance, and so on.

Plot

Melody is really excited when she finally gets her talking board and spends hours learning how to customize it to her wants and needs. Create a mock talking board that includes the words you would want if you couldn't speak.

Teacher Plans

Vocabulary Overview

Ten key words from this section are provided below with definitions and sentences about how the words are used in the book. Choose one of the vocabulary activity sheets (pages 25 or 26) for students to complete as they read this section. Monitor students as they work to ensure the definitions they have found are accurate and relate to the text. Finally, discuss these important vocabulary words with students. If you think these words or other words in the section warrant more time devoted to them, there are suggestions in the introduction for other vocabulary activities (page 5).

Word	Definition	Sentence about Text
tentative (ch. 8)	hesitant; halting	At first the dog's barks are soft and **tentative**, getting louder when Mom doesn't check on Melody.
statistically (ch. 9)	based on numbers; statistics	Dad tries telling Mom that, **statistically**, their next baby should be fine.
paparazzi (ch. 9)	aggressive photographers of famous people	Dad takes so many photographs of Penny that he looks like one of the **paparazzi**!
obsession (ch. 10)	something you think about all the time	Melody's little sister has an **obsession** with hats.
interact (ch. 11)	mingle; mix	The new class gives Melody a chance to **interact** with more students.
mimicked (ch. 11)	imitated; copied	The teacher punishes the girls after they **mimicked** Willy.
influence (ch. 11)	the power to change or affect someone or something	Mrs. Lovelace believes that music can **influence** people.
outcasts (ch. 11)	outsiders; interlopers	Melody is excited that the little group of **outcasts** will be going to music class each week.
contentedly (ch. 11)	happily; cheerfully	Jill sits **contentedly** next to a fellow student.
evasively (ch. 13)	avoid answering directly	Rose answers Claire's question **evasively**.

Name _____ _____

Date _____ _____

Understanding Vocabulary Words

Directions: The following words appear in this section of the book. Use context clues and reference materials to determine an accurate definition for each word.

Word	Definition
tentative (ch. 8)	
statistically (ch. 9)	
paparazzi (ch. 9)	
obsession (ch. 10)	
interact (ch. 11)	
mimicked (ch. 11)	
influence (ch. 11)	
outcasts (ch. 11)	
contentedly (ch. 11)	
evasively (ch. 13)	

Name _____

Date _____

During-Reading Vocabulary Activity

Directions: As you read these chapters, record at least eight important words on the lines below. Try to find interesting, difficult, intriguing, special, or funny words. Your words can be long or short. They can be hard or easy to spell. After each word, use context clues in the text and reference materials to define the word.

- _____
- _____
- _____
- _____
- _____
- _____
- _____
- _____
- _____

Directions: Respond to these questions about the words in this section.

1. Why does Melody say that Penny has a hat **obsession**?

   _____

   _____

2. Describe the ways music can **influence** people according to Mrs. Lovelace.

   _____

   _____

    © Shell Education

Analyzing the Literature

Provided below are discussion questions you can use in small groups, with the whole class, or for written assignments. Each question is given at two levels so you can choose the right question for each group of students. Activity sheets with these questions are provided (pages 28–29) if you want students to write their responses. For each question, a few key discussion points are provided for your reference.

Story Element	■ Level 1	▲ Level 2	Key Discussion Points
Plot	Why is Melody so frustrated over Ollie's death?	How is Ollie's jumping out of the bowl an important symbol for Melody's life?	Melody is blamed for Ollie's death because she can't explain what really happened. Ollie's jumping out of his bowl symbolizes Melody's life because she feels trapped in her body just like Ollie is trapped in the bowl.
Character	In chapter 8, we learn that Melody likes country-western music. What does she see and smell when she listens to it?	Describe Melody's reactions to the music before and after Ollie jumps from the bowl. Why do they change?	Melody says the music sounds orangey and yellowish, and she smells lemons. It makes her mellow as she watches Ollie swim. After he jumps, she no longer sees the colors.
Plot	How does life change for Melody after Butterscotch arrives? After Penny arrives?	Compare life before and after Butterscotch arrives. What conflicting feelings does Melody have about the baby?	Butterscotch is helpful and can sense when Melody needs comfort and someone to communicate for her. Melody worries that Penny will take even more time than she does, although Penny turns out to be a good baby.
Setting	Compare Melody's old wheelchair with her new one. What are the pros and cons of each?	What impact does the electric wheelchair have on Melody's attitude about school, especially about the inclusion classes?	The new wheelchair is much heavier, making it difficult for Melody to get places. However, she has more freedom at school. She can handle it herself instead of relying on an adult to move her around. She can get to and from classes more easily. She can be out in the halls, around other kids.

Name _____

Date _____

Analyzing the Literature

Directions: Think about the section you just read. Read each question, and state your response with textual evidence.

1. Why is Melody so frustrated over Ollie's death?

   _____

   _____

   _____

   _____

2. In chapter 8, we learn that Melody likes country-western music. What does she see and smell when she listens to it?

   _____

   _____

   _____

   _____

3. How does life change for Melody after Butterscotch arrives? After Penny arrives?

   _____

   _____

   _____

   _____

4. Compare Melody's old wheelchair with her new one. What are the pros and cons of each?

   _____

   _____

   _____

Name _____

Date _____

▲ Analyzing the Literature

Directions: Think about the section you just read. Read each question, and state your response with textual evidence.

1. How is Ollie's jumping out of the bowl an important symbol for Melody's life?

    _____

    _____

    _____

    _____

2. Describe Melody's reactions to the music before and after Ollie jumps from the bowl. Why do they change?

    _____

    _____

    _____

    _____

3. Compare life before and after Butterscotch arrives. What conflicting feelings does Melody have about the baby?

    _____

    _____

    _____

    _____

4. What impact does the electric wheelchair have on Melody's attitude about school, especially about the inclusion classes?

    _____

    _____

    _____

Name _____

Date _____

Reader Response

Directions: Choose one of the following prompts about this section to answer. Be sure you include a topic sentence in your response, use textual evidence to support your opinion, and provide a strong conclusion that summarizes your opinion.

Writing Prompts

- **Opinion/Argument Piece**—Think about the limitations that Melody faces as they are described in this section. Give at least three examples. Choose the limitation that you think would be most difficult to live with, and explain why you think it is difficult.

- **Informative/Explanatory Piece**—In chapter 12, Melody gets an aide. Describe the impact Catherine has on Melody's school life. Use examples from the text to support your answer.

_____

_____

_____

_____

_____

_____

_____

_____

_____

_____

_____

_____

Name _____

Date _____

Close Reading the Literature

Directions: Closely reread the beginning of chapter 13, ending with, "If she has thorns like real roses do, I've never noticed." Read each question, and then revisit the text to find evidence that supports your answer.

1. Melody says that an artist would love this early November day. What examples in the text support Melody's thoughts about the day?

   _____

   _____

   _____

2. Explain why Dad says he won't be able to afford Penny when she is old enough to go shopping. What does she do that prompts his statement?

   _____

   _____

   _____

3. Melody says, "I wish I had enough coordination to have 'attitude!'" What does Melody say or do that explains her feelings about Penny when she says this?

   _____

   _____

   _____

4. Melody has another wish—to use crayons. Drawing examples from the passage, explain what Melody would do with crayons and why.

   _____

   _____

   _____

Name _____

Date _____

Making Connections—Make Your Case!

Directions: It takes years for Melody to get a mobility assistant, an aide dedicated to helping her. Mrs. Shannon says that budget issues cause the delay. Write a letter that makes a case for providing funds for an important issue your classroom or school faces. Decide who should receive the letter—your principal, school superintendent, or editor of a local newspaper. Make a convincing argument for your case!

Dear _____ ,

_____

_____

_____

_____

_____

_____

_____

_____

_____

_____

_____

_____

_____

Sincerely,

_____

© Shell Education

Name _____ _____

Date _____

Creating with the Story Elements

Directions: Thinking about the story elements of character, setting, and plot in a novel is very important to understanding what is happening and why. Complete **one** of the following activities based on what you've read so far. Be creative and have fun!

Characters

Design a hat and outfit that two-year-old Penny would like to wear.

Setting

Thanks to her new wheelchair and the inclusion classes, fifth grade is much better for Melody. Write a description or make a detailed, labeled drawing of the ideal classroom for a person in a wheelchair.

Plot

Melody is very excited about going to the aquarium. The actual experience, though, is somewhat like climbing a mountain—there are ups and downs. Make a chart or other labeled design that describes the highs and lows.

Teacher Plans

Vocabulary Overview

Ten key words from this section are provided below with definitions and sentences about how the words are used in the book. Choose one of the vocabulary activity sheets (pages 35 or 36) for students to complete as they read this section. Monitor students as they work to ensure the definitions they have found are accurate and relate to the text. Finally, discuss these important vocabulary words with students. If you think these words or other words in the section warrant more time devoted to them, there are suggestions in the introduction for other vocabulary activities (page 5).

Word	Definition	Sentence about Text
accumulate (ch. 15)	collect; gather	The students watch the snow **accumulate** on the grass and trees.
tradition (ch. 15)	custom; practice	Mrs. Shannon explains the **tradition** of decorating a snowman.
petulant (ch. 17)	sullen; cranky	Claire is **petulant** and disbelieving when she realizes Melody might be smarter than she thought.
rallied (ch. 17)	united; encouraged	Mr. Dimming **rallies** the class like a football team for the Whiz Kids tryouts.
indignation (ch. 18)	outrage; anger	Mrs. V gets so upset with Melody that she lets her **indignation** show.
stifle (ch. 18)	smother; cover	Rose tries to **stifle** her laugh, but all the other kids laugh out loud.
tidbits (ch. 18)	pieces; bits	Mrs. V is going to help Melody study thousands of **tidbits** of information.
energized (ch. 18)	eager; excited	The studying tires Melody, but she also feels **energized** by it.
convulsion (ch. 18)	seizure; attack	No one comes to check on Melody, not even to see if she's having a **convulsion** or spazzing out.
ambling (ch. 19)	strolling; wandering	Penny is **ambling** down the sidewalk when Mom stops her.

Name _____

Date _____

Understanding Vocabulary Words

Directions: The following words appear in this section of the book. Use context clues and reference materials to determine an accurate definition for each word.

Word	Definition
accumulate (ch. 15)	
tradition (ch. 15)	
petulant (ch. 17)	
rallied (ch. 17)	
indignation (ch. 18)	
stifle (ch. 18)	
tidbits (ch. 18)	
energized (ch. 18)	
convulsion (ch. 18)	
ambling (ch. 19)	

Name _____

Date _____

During-Reading Vocabulary Activity

Directions: As you read these chapters, record at least eight important words on the lines below. Try to find interesting, difficult, intriguing, special, or funny words. Your words can be long or short. They can be hard or easy to spell. After each word, use context clues in the text and reference materials to define the word.

- _____

- _____

- _____

- _____

- _____

- _____

- _____

- _____

- _____

- _____

Directions: Now, organize your words. Rewrite each of your words on a sticky note. Work as a group to create a bar graph of your words. You should stack any words that are the same on top of one another. Different words appear in different columns. Finally, discuss with a group why certain words were chosen more often than other words.

Analyzing the Literature

Provided below are discussion questions you can use in small groups, with the whole class, or for written assignments. Each question is given at two levels so you can choose the right question for each group of students. Activity sheets with these questions are provided (pages 38–39) if you want students to write their responses. For each question, a few key discussion points are provided for your reference.

Story Element	■ Level 1	▲ Level 2	Key Discussion Points
Plot	What idea does Melody get from seeing Rose with her laptop?	Explain why it is significant for Melody to have the idea of getting a computer.	Melody realizes that she could work a computer. She also could communicate if she had the right computer. For someone who has had little opportunity to participate in a group, this is important. Melody will also be able to learn more quickly and show what she knows.
Character	What role does Mrs. V play after the computer comes?	Describe the partnership between Melody and Mrs. V after the computer arrives. How do they work together?	Mrs. V inputs a lot of words and phrases for the computer. She ensures that Melody gets time to practice, and Melody shows her appreciation. Mrs. V convinces Melody to wait until she's skilled before taking it to school. She also shares in the joy of Melody having more control over her life and learning.
Setting	Melody brings her computer to language arts class in chapter 16. How do the students react at first?	There are mixed reactions to Melody's computer in the language arts class. Why is Connor's reaction so important?	Most of the students are intrigued by the computer. Connor, a leader, has given his approval, and most students follow his lead. Claire tries to put Melody down, but Mrs. Gordon stops her.
Character	How do the students react to Melody getting a perfect score on the test?	Melody isn't thrilled with getting a perfect score on the test. In what ways does she act out because of this? Is her behavior justified?	The students are disbelieving. Some claim she cheated. Most laugh, too. Melody is hurt because she realizes they think she is "messed up." She is mean to her little sister when she gets home.

Name _____

Date _____

Analyzing the Literature

Directions: Think about the section you just read. Read each question, and state your response with textual evidence.

1. What idea does Melody get from seeing Rose with her laptop?

_____

_____

_____

_____

2. What role does Mrs. V play after the computer comes?

_____

_____

_____

_____

3. Melody brings her computer to language arts class in chapter 16. How do the students react at first?

_____

_____

_____

_____

4. How do the students react to Melody getting a perfect score on the test?

_____

_____

_____

_____

Name _____

Date _____

▲ Analyzing the Literature

Directions: Think about the section you just read. Read each question, and state your response with textual evidence.

1. Explain why it is significant for Melody to have the idea of getting a computer.

   _____

   _____

   _____

   _____

2. Describe the partnership between Melody and Mrs. V after the computer arrives. How do they work together?

   _____

   _____

   _____

   _____

3. There are mixed reactions to Melody's computer in the language arts class. Why is Connor's reaction so important?

   _____

   _____

   _____

   _____

4. Melody isn't thrilled with getting a perfect score on the test. In what ways does she act out because of this? Is her behavior justified?

   _____

   _____

   _____

Name _____

Date _____

Reader Response

Directions: Choose one of the following prompts about this section to answer. Be sure you include a topic sentence in your response, use textual evidence to support your opinion, and provide a strong conclusion that summarizes your opinion.

Writing Prompts

- **Narrative Piece**—Mr. Dimming seems to be a good teacher, but he also doesn't seem to "get" Melody. Compare examples from the story to times you have felt that a teacher or other adult hasn't fully understood you.
- **Opinion/Argument Piece**—Melody has a keen mind. She also has a terrific sense of humor. Choose which trait you think is more important for a person to have—great intelligence or great humor. Use examples from the story to support your position.

_____

_____

_____

_____

_____

_____

_____

_____

_____

_____

_____

_____

_____

                    © *Shell Education*

Close Reading the Literature

Directions: Closely reread from the beginning of chapter 19, ending with, "And you *will* fly on Monday when you take the test." Read each question, and then revisit the text to find evidence that supports your answer.

1. What can you infer from the first paragraph of the section? Justify your answer with evidence from the text.

   _____

   _____

   _____

2. Find an example in the passage that showcases Melody's ability to prepare for interactions with different kinds of people. Explain what it shows about Melody's personality.

   _____

   _____

   _____

3. What connection between the setting and the mood does the author establish in this part of the story?

   _____

   _____

   _____

4. Explain why Mrs. V tells Melody that she is a bird. Include examples from the text to support your answer.

   _____

   _____

   _____

Name _____

Date _____

Making Connections–Solve a Problem

Directions: Melody has to face some big obstacles due to cerebral palsy. She can't talk or get around without help. There are some people who face smaller obstacles, such as balance issues or being weak. Design something that could help people who have limitations or challenges. It could be a game, activity, invention, or tool. Draw your invention, and describe who it helps and how.

_____

_____

_____

_____

_____

_____

_____

_____

© Shell Education

Name _____

Date _____

Creating with the Story Elements

Directions: Thinking about the story elements of character, setting, and plot in a novel is very important to understanding what is happening and why. Complete **one** of the following activities based on what you've read so far. Be creative, and have fun!

Characters

Mrs. V refers to Melody as a bird. Draw a bird that is symbolic of Melody. Think about the colors she likes, her appreciation for clothes, her intelligence, and her sense of humor. Make the bird represent Melody's spirit.

Setting

Reread chapter 19. Draw the winter scene as it is described by Melody. Be sure to include the details she mentions, such as the flowers and the wisps of clouds in the sky.

Plot

Imagine Mr. Dimming has written to an advice columnist because he is not sure he believes that a student with cerebral palsy can be so smart. Write an answer to him as the advice columnist.

Vocabulary Overview

Ten key words from this section are provided below with definitions and sentences about how the words are used in the book. Choose one of the vocabulary activity sheets (pages 45 or 46) for students to complete as they read this section. Monitor students as they work to ensure the definitions they have found are accurate and relate to the text. Finally, discuss these important vocabulary words with students. If you think these words or other words in the section warrant more time devoted to them, there are suggestions in the introduction for other vocabulary activities (page 5).

Word	Definition	Sentence about Text
alternates (ch. 21)	substitutes; stand-ins	Molly can't believe that she is one of the **alternates** instead of on the team.
mandatory (ch. 21)	required	Practice is **mandatory** for the students on the Whiz Kids team.
negativity (ch. 23)	pessimism; lack of enthusiasm	Melody decides to ignore Molly's **negativity** and not worry so much.
moderator (ch. 24)	person in charge of a meeting or game	The **moderator** gives everyone instructions about the competition's rules.
modulated (ch. 24)	controlled and pleasant to listen to	Mr. Kingsley's **modulated** voice keeps the attention of the audience.
represent (ch. 24)	stand for; act for	The winning team **represents** the state in the national competition.
chaperones (ch. 24)	adults who attend an event to ensure safety and good behavior	The winning team and its **chaperones** get to go to Washington, D.C., for the competition and some sightseeing.
bistro (ch. 26)	small, informal restaurant	Connor suggests that the team go to a **bistro** after the competition.
enthusiastically (ch. 26)	willingly; eagerly	The students and Mr. Dimming talk **enthusiastically** about the events for the trip.
incident (ch. 26)	happening; occurrence	Melody wonders if Claire is upset over the embarrassing **incident** in the restaurant.

Name _____

Date _____

Understanding Vocabulary Words

Directions: The following words appear in this section of the book. Use context clues and reference materials to determine an accurate definition for each word.

Word	Definition
alternates (ch. 21)	
mandatory (ch. 21)	
negativity (ch. 23)	
moderator (ch. 24)	
modulated (ch. 24)	
represent (ch. 24)	
chaperones (ch. 24)	
bistro (ch. 26)	
enthusiastically (ch. 26)	
incident (ch. 26)	

Name _____

Date _____

During-Reading Vocabulary Activity

Directions: As you read these chapters, record at least eight important words on the lines below. Try to find interesting, difficult, intriguing, special, or funny words. Your words can be long or short. They can be hard or easy to spell. After each word, use context clues in the text and reference materials to define the word.

- _____
- _____
- _____
- _____
- _____
- _____
- _____
- _____
- _____

Directions: Respond to these questions about the words in this section.

1. Why does Mr. Dimming make practices **mandatory** for the team members?

_____

_____

2. Why doesn't anyone want to mention the **incident** at the restaurant?

_____

_____

          © Shell Education

Analyzing the Literature

Provided below are discussion questions you can use in small groups, with the whole class, or for written assignments. Each question is given at two levels so you can choose the right question for each group of students. Activity sheets with these questions are provided (pages 48–49) if you want students to write their responses. For each question, a few key discussion points are provided for your reference.

Story Element	■ Level 1	▲ Level 2	Key Discussion Points
Character	Why does Melody want to leave the room after she's learned that she's on the team?	After learning she is on the team, Melody says, "There was the team, and there was me." What does she mean?	Melody knows that she can do well in the competition, but she also knows that some of the students will resent her or find her presence off-putting. She doesn't feel like a true member of the team because of the resentment by some. She has mixed feelings, but she still shows up for practice.
Setting	Describe the television studio where the competition is held.	How does the stage manager make the television studio more manageable for Melody? What motivates him?	The area of the competition is brightly lit, with a separate room behind the cameras for the audience. Paul, the stage manager, has rigged a special answer board for Melody, one with large buttons. He has a son in a wheelchair, and he is used to making accommodations.
Plot	What happens during the television interview after the team wins?	Claire claims to be Melody's friend during the interview. What motivates her to lie? How would you react to Claire?	A lot of attention gets paid to Melody because she's a member of the team. She handles the questions well. Claire is undoubtedly resentful of the attention Melody gets. Claire wants to make herself look good, so she claims to be Melody's friend.
Character	Why is Melody embarrassed at the restaurant?	Compare Melody's embarrassment of being fed to Claire's getting sick. Which person has the tougher experience?	Melody feels embarrassed because she has to be pushed up the stairs and because she has to be spoon-fed by her mom at the table. Opinions will vary about which experience was worse.

Name _____

Date _____

Analyzing the Literature

Directions: Think about the section you just read. Read each question, and state your response with textual evidence.

1. Why does Melody want to leave the room after she's learned that she's on the team?

   _____

   _____

   _____

   _____

2. Describe the television studio where the competition is held.

   _____

   _____

   _____

   _____

3. What happens during the television interview after the team wins?

   _____

   _____

   _____

   _____

4. Why is Melody embarrassed at the restaurant?

   _____

   _____

   _____

   _____

    © Shell Education

Name _____ _____

Date _____

▲ Analyzing the Literature

Directions: Think about the section you just read. Read each question, and state your response with textual evidence.

1. After learning she is on the team, Melody says, "There was the team, and there was me." What does she mean?

   _____

   _____

   _____

   _____

2. How does the stage manager make the television studio more manageable for Melody? What motivates him?

   _____

   _____

   _____

   _____

3. Claire claims to be Melody's friend during the interview. What motivates her to lie? How would you react to Claire?

   _____

   _____

   _____

4. Compare Melody's embarrassment of being fed to Claire's getting sick. Which person has the tougher experience?

   _____

   _____

   _____

Name _____

Date _____

Reader Response

Directions: Choose one of the following prompts about this section to answer. Be sure you include a topic sentence in your response, use textual evidence to support your opinion, and provide a strong conclusion that summarizes your opinion.

Writing Prompts

- **Narrative Piece**—Discuss Mr. Dimming's attitude about Melody's participation on the team. Describe how his previous treatment of Melody has changed. Predict whether or not he will be fully supportive of Melody as the competition moves forward to the finals.

- **Opinion/Argument Piece**—Think about Claire's behavior during this section of the book. Does she get what she deserves at the restaurant? Or does she deserve a worse punishment? Justify your response using details from the story.

_____

_____

_____

_____

_____

_____

_____

_____

_____

_____

_____

_____

Name _____

Date _____

Close Reading the Literature

Directions: Closely reread the first section of chapter 26. Stop reading with, "Then we finally rolled into the dining room, which was crowded with noisy, laughing customers." Read each question, and then revisit the text to find evidence that supports your answer.

1. What can you infer about Mr. Dimming's opinion of Connor after Connor recommends that they go to Linguini's?

   _____

   _____

   _____

2. Use the text to explain what convinces Melody that she should go with the team to Linguini's. What makes her feel as though her balloon has been popped?

   _____

   _____

   _____

3. Why do you think Melody doesn't want the waiter to carry her up the stairs?

   _____

   _____

   _____

4. How does the author show the effort needed to get Melody into the restaurant? Include words or lines from the text to support your answer.

   _____

   _____

   _____

Name _____

Date _____

Making Connections—In Melody's Place

Directions: Many public places have made changes to accommodate wheelchairs, but others have not. Choose an area to evaluate through Melody's eyes. It could be your school playground, the mall, or any other place that you regularly visit. Make a list of 10 features, such as sidewalks, stairs, or the height of water fountains. Rank them on a scale of 1 (poor) to 5 (great) of accessibility for those in wheelchairs. Include recommendations for improvements.

The area I evaluated was _____ .

Feature	1 (poor) to 5 (great)	Recommendations

    © Shell Education

Name _____

Date _____

Creating with the Story Elements

Directions: Thinking about the story elements of character, setting, and plot in a novel is very important to understanding what is happening and why. Complete **one** of the following activities based on what you've read so far. Be creative, and have fun!

Characters

Molly and Claire sometimes act like "mean girls." Make a reading list of five or more recommended books that might help them gain more empathy.

Setting

Draw the set of the Whiz Kids regional competition. Be sure to include Melody and the rest of the Spaulding Street Elementary team members. Use the text's descriptions to help you.

Plot

Write a newspaper article based on the interview described in chapter 25. Include a drawing or picture you would want to include with the article.

Teacher Plans

Vocabulary Overview

Ten key words from this section are provided below with definitions and sentences about how the words are used in the book. Choose one of the vocabulary activity sheets (pages 55 or 56) for students to complete as they read this section. Monitor students as they work to ensure the definitions they have found are accurate and relate to the text. Finally, discuss these important vocabulary words with students. If you think these words or other words in the section warrant more time devoted to them, there are suggestions in the introduction for other vocabulary activities (page 5).

Word	Definition	Sentence about Text
outrage (ch. 28)	indignation; anger	Claire shows her **outrage** when she complains about the team.
smug (ch. 28)	self-satisfied; self-assured	Molly looks **smug** when she finds out she beat Claire by two points.
devastated (ch. 29)	shattered; very upset	Melody feels **devastated** when the team leaves her behind.
plaintively (ch. 29)	sadly; sorrowfully	Mom can't hide her distress as she talks **plaintively** to Melody.
hustle (ch. 30)	hurry; rush	Dad tries to **hustle** Melody out to the bus on time.
grumpily (ch. 30)	crossly; crankily	Mom **grumpily** agrees to go to work on her day off.
tension (ch. 31)	strain; stress	Mrs. V massages Melody's back and shoulders until the **tension** melts away.
resilient (ch. 31)	able to recover quickly	Mrs. V assures Melody that toddlers are **resilient** and that Penny will be just fine.
envious (ch. 32)	jealous; resentful	Freddy feels **envious** about Melody's trip, wishing he could have gone.
ballistic (ch. 32)	extremely upset; furious	Melody resists going **ballistic** in spite of being angry.

© Shell Education

Name _____

Date _____

Understanding Vocabulary Words

Directions: The following words appear in this section of the book. Use context clues and reference materials to determine an accurate definition for each word.

Word	Definition
outrage (ch. 28)	
smug (ch. 28)	
devastated (ch. 29)	
plaintively (ch. 29)	
hustle (ch. 30)	
grumpily (ch. 30)	
tension (ch. 31)	
resilient (ch. 31)	
envious (ch. 32)	
ballistic (ch. 32)	

Name _____

Date _____

During-Reading Vocabulary Activity

Directions: As you read these chapters, choose five important words from the story. Then, use those five words to complete this word flow chart. On each arrow, write a vocabulary word. In the boxes between the words, explain how the words connect. An example for the words *tension* and *resilient* has been done for you.

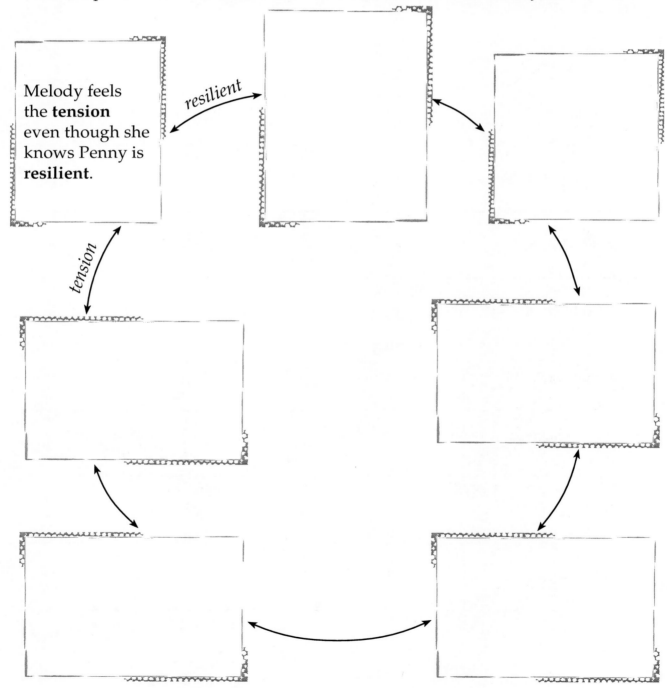

Melody feels the **tension** even though she knows Penny is **resilient**.

resilient

tension

© *Shell Education*

Analyzing the Literature

Provided below are discussion questions you can use in small groups, with the whole class, or for written assignments. Each question is given at two levels so you can choose the right question for each group of students. Activity sheets with these questions are provided (pages 58–59) if you want students to write their responses. For each question, a few key discussion points are provided for your reference.

Story Element	■ Level 1	▲ Level 2	Key Discussion Points
Character	How does Catherine counteract Melody's negative feelings about the competition in chapter 27?	Being an aide requires wisdom, patience, and humor. Find examples of each as Catherine deals with Melody in chapter 27.	Catherine reminds Melody that the team needs her for their success. Catherine agrees that Melody might drool, but she says to pack tissues. She makes Melody laugh by pointing out that Connor farts sometimes. She even scolds Melody slightly, telling her to stop feeling sorry for herself.
Setting	What keeps Melody from going to Washington, D.C., after she arrives at the airport?	Which is most significant in keeping Melody from going to Washington, D.C.: the snowstorm, the team not inviting her to breakfast, or the team not calling her?	A snowstorm means that the flights have been canceled, and Melody cannot get to Washington, D.C. Opinions will vary about the significance of the events. Discuss why it is unfair to exclude her from breakfast as well as not to call her from the airport.
Plot	What circumstances trigger Penny's injury?	Compare what happens to Penny with the fish that jumps from the bowl. What important message do the events give the reader?	The accident is due to a series of events: the family being tired and sad, Melody's inability to effectively communicate, and bad luck. The accident underscores the frustration felt by Melody due to being unable to communicate effectively or to control certain aspects of her life, just as the fish jumping from the bowl did.
Plot	How does Melody handle herself when she confronts the class for leaving her?	Why does Melody laugh when she is given the trophy?	Melody doesn't go ballistic. She remains calm when she confronts her teammates. When they hand her the trophy as a peace offering, she laughs and knocks the trophy off her tray. She essentially doesn't accept their half-hearted attempts at an apology.

Name _____

Date _____

■ Analyzing the Literature

Directions: Think about the section you just read. Read each question, and state your response with textual evidence.

1. How does Catherine counteract Melody's negative feelings about the competition in chapter 27?

_____

_____

_____

_____

2. What keeps Melody from going to Washington, D.C., after she arrives at the airport?

_____

_____

_____

_____

3. What circumstances trigger Penny's injury?

_____

_____

_____

4. How does Melody handle herself when she confronts the class for leaving her?

_____

_____

_____

Name _____

Date _____

▲ Analyzing the Literature

Directions: Think about the section you just read. Read each question, and state your response with textual evidence.

1. Being an aide requires wisdom, patience, and humor. Find examples of each as Catherine deals with Melody in chapter 27.

   _____

   _____

   _____

   _____

2. Which is most significant in keeping Melody from going to Washington, D.C.: the snowstorm, the team not inviting her to breakfast, or the team not calling her?

   _____

   _____

   _____

   _____

3. Compare what happens to Penny with the fish that jumps from the bowl. What important message do the events give the reader?

   _____

   _____

   _____

4. Why does Melody laugh when she is given the trophy?

   _____

   _____

   _____

Name _____

Date _____

Reader Response

Directions: Choose one of the following prompts about this section to answer. Be sure you include a topic sentence in your response, use textual evidence to support your opinion, and provide a strong conclusion that summarizes your opinion.

Writing Prompts

- **Opinion/Argument Piece**—The other kids don't seem happy that Melody is the only one pictured in the newspaper. Do the other kids have a right to be upset about this? Why or why not?
- **Narrative Piece**—Describe what you think Melody will be like in sixth grade. Identify the important lessons she has learned throughout the story and predict how she'll put them to good use.

_____

_____

_____

_____

_____

_____

_____

_____

_____

_____

_____

_____

_____

Name _____

Date _____

Close Reading the Literature

Directions: Closely reread chapter 33. Read each question, and then revisit the text to find evidence that supports your answer.

1. In what ways is Melody like other fifth graders? Use examples from the text to support your answer.

   _____

   _____

   _____

2. The author uses the goldfish and the bird as symbols of Melody's life. Using examples from the text, explain why a puzzle without the box is another good symbol.

   _____

   _____

   _____

3. Melody says that her family, even Butterscotch, is spoiling Penny, but she doesn't mind. Why do you think this doesn't bother Melody?

   _____

   _____

   _____

4. The author concludes by repeating the first few paragraphs of the book. Reread the section that begins with *"Words."* Then, think about the title, *Out of My Mind*. What is the significance of the title? Support your answer with examples from Melody's autobiography.

   _____

   _____

   _____

Name _____

Date _____

Making Connections–Character Report Card

Directions: Complete the report card for each character's behavior, giving grades of *A, B, C, D,* or *F.* For example, a character that shows strength of character and makes consistently good decisions would receive an *A.* Then, write a sentence justifying your choice in the Comments column. Melody's is done as an example.

Name of Character	Grade	Comments
Melody	A	Melody tries hard, uses humor effectively, and is not easily discouraged.
Mom		
Dad		
Mr. Dimming		
Mrs. V		
Catherine		
Molly		
Claire		
Rose		

    © Shell Education

Name _____

Date _____

Creating with the Story Elements

Directions: Thinking about the story elements of character, setting, and plot in a novel is very important to understanding what is happening and why. Complete **one** of the following activities based on what you've read so far. Be creative, and have fun!

Characters

Choose one of the students and create a scrapbook page that represents the fifth grade year. You can draw and use cutouts from magazines, newspapers, or printouts from the Internet to illustrate the page.

Setting

Design a new cover for the book, one that symbolizes Melody's world, either *in* or *out* of her mind.

Plot

Brainstorm alternative endings of the book with a friend. Outline the last few chapters, and write the last two paragraphs as you would have ended the book.

© Shell Education

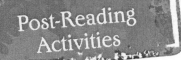

Name _____

Date _____

Post-Reading Theme Thoughts

Directions: Read each of the statements in the first column. Choose a main character from *Out of My Mind*. Think about that character's point of view. From that character's perspective, decide if the character would agree or disagree with the statements. Record the character's opinion by marking an X in Agree or Disagree for each statement. Explain your choices in the fourth column using text evidence.

Character I Chose: _____

Statement	Agree	Disagree	Explain Your Answer
A person who can't talk probably isn't very smart.			
People who have learning disabilities should attend special classes so they don't slow down the rest of the students.			
A person who has a hard time with a school subject just needs to study harder.			
All students should take tests in the same way so that it's fair for everyone.			

    © Shell Education

Name _____

Date _____

Culminating Activity: Surrounded by Words

Directions: Melody chooses interesting, unusual, and intriguing words to open and close her story. List 10 words that tell about you. Choose a symbol that represents the words, such as Melody's snowflakes, and draw it at the bottom of the page. (Other ideas might include raindrops, balloons, rocks, or flowers.) Make the words and symbol representative of *you*.

- _____   • _____

- _____   • _____

- _____   • _____

- _____   • _____

- _____   • _____

My Symbol

Name _____

Date _____

Culminating Activity: Surrounded by Words (cont.)

Directions: Create a poem using some of the words you generated on the previous page. Consider writing an acrostic poem, a haiku, a cinquain, a diamante, a tanka, or a concrete poem. Make the poem representative of *you*.

_____

_____

_____

_____

_____

_____

_____

_____

_____

_____

_____

_____

_____

_____

Name _____

Date _____

Comprehension Assessment

Directions: Circle the letter for the best response to each question.

1. What is the meaning of *potential* as it is used in the book?
    A. growth
    B. chance
    C. attitude
    D. capability

2. Which detail from the book best supports your answer to question 1?
    E. "Well, the whole thing was almost a disaster."
    F. "We were going to be in a *regular* classroom!"
    G. "All of the 'normal' children in the music class ... turned to stare."
    H. "I tried to raise my hand, but she didn't notice me."

3. Write the main idea of the text below in the graphic organizer.

   "I close my eyes, trying not to cry, dreaming of the perfect Melody-made computer. First of all, it would talk! Oh, yes. People would have to tell me to shut up! And it would have room to store *all* my words, not just the most common ones that have gotten pasted on my dumb plastic board."

   ┌───┐
   │ **Main Idea (question 3)**   │
   │   │
   └───┘

   Details (question 4)   **Details (question 4)**

Comprehension Assessment (cont.)

4. Choose **two** supporting details from those below to add to the graphic organizer on the previous page.

   E. Melody likes to watch documentaries and films.

   F. Melody realizes that Stephen Hawking uses a computer.

   G. Computers can be adapted for users with special needs.

   H. Rose can use her computer for doing homework.

5. Which statement best expresses the central theme of the book?

   A. Face every day with a sense of humor.

   B. Winning requires having a good attitude.

   C. Don't let your disability interfere with your ability.

   D. You can be happy if you really try.

6. Which statement provides the best evidence for your answer to number 5?

   E. Melody: "It limits my body, but not my mind."

   F. Melody: "Afraid it would feel so good, I'd just fly away."

   G. Mrs. V: "We have to figure out what's in her head."

   H. Mom: "You're going to rock on Monday!"

7. What is the purpose of these sentences from when Melody confronts the class: "Mr. Dimming clears his throat. He shifts from one foot to the other. He runs his finger around the collar of his dim white shirt."

   _____

   _____

   _____

8. Which other quotation serves a similar purpose as the one in number 7?

   A. "No one seems to know what to say."

   B. "I am amazingly calm."

   C. "At last I break the silence."

   D. "I don't react at all. I just wait."

Name _____

Date _____

Response to Literature: State Your Mind

Some people think that kids with physical or mental challenges should be sent to special schools. They think that having specialized teachers will serve them better. Other people think that public schools are better even if they are more complicated. Like Melody's parents, they believe public schools give their children the best possible chance at learning.

Directions: Think about what you have learned from reading *Out of My Mind*. How would you advocate for students with special needs? Write an essay that describes how you think students with challenges should be educated.

Write an essay that follows these guidelines:

- State your opinion about the importance of mainstream education.
- Write at least 750 words.
- Include main points, such as those listed in the directions above.
- Draw upon what you learned from reading *Out of My Mind*.
- Provide a conclusion that summarizes your point of view.

Final essays are due on _____.

Name _____

Date _____

Response to Literature Rubric

Directions: Use this rubric to evaluate student responses.

	Exceptional Writing	Quality Writing	Developing Writing
Focus and Organization	☐ States a clear opinion and elaborates well. Engages readers from the opening hook through the middle to the conclusion. Demonstrates clear understanding of the intended audience and purpose of the piece.	☐ Provides a clear and consistent opinion. Maintains a clear perspective and supports it through elaborating details. Makes the opinion clear in the opening hook and summarizes well in the conclusion.	☐ Provides an inconsistent point of view. Does not support the topic adequately or misses pertinent information. Lacks clarity in the beginning, middle, and conclusion.
Text Evidence	☐ Provides comprehensive and accurate support. Includes relevant and worthwhile text references.	☐ Provides limited support. Provides few supporting text references.	☐ Provides very limited support for the text. Provides no supporting text references.
Written Expression	☐ Uses descriptive and precise language with clarity and intention. Maintains a consistent voice and uses an appropriate tone that supports meaning. Uses multiple sentence types and transitions well between ideas.	☐ Uses a broad vocabulary. Maintains a consistent voice and supports a tone and feelings through language. Varies sentence length and word choices.	☐ Uses a limited and unvaried vocabulary. Provides an inconsistent or weak voice and tone. Provides little to no variation in sentence type and length.
Language Conventions	☐ Capitalizes, punctuates, and spells accurately. Demonstrates complete thoughts within sentences, with accurate subject-verb agreement. Uses paragraphs appropriately and with clear purpose.	☐ Capitalizes, punctuates, and spells accurately. Demonstrates complete thoughts within sentences and appropriate grammar. Paragraphs are properly divided and supported.	☐ Incorrectly capitalizes, punctuates, and spells. Uses fragmented or run-on sentences. Utilizes poor grammar overall. Paragraphs are poorly divided and developed.

© Shell Education

The responses provided here are just examples of what the students may answer. Many accurate responses are possible for the questions throughout this unit.

During-Reading Vocabulary Activity—Section 1: Chapters 1–7 (page 16)

1. Dr. Hugely describes Melody as being "severely brain-damaged and profoundly retarded" in his **evaluation**.

2. Mrs. Billups believes that parents of special needs children are not always realistic and are often **exaggerating** when they discuss what their children are able to do.

Close Reading the Literature—Section 1: Chapters 1–7 (page 21)

1. Melody plays games, runs, does gymnastics, square-dances, talks with her friends, whispers secrets, and sings in her dreams. When she wakes up, she is let down as reality sets in, and she has to be fed and dressed and go to school.

2. Melody thinks they should get paid a million dollars. They have to take care of the special students: bathroom needs, feeding, etc. Melody thinks their job is hard and that most people don't realize it.

3. Mrs. Tracy figures out that Melody likes books and has her listen to audiobooks. She pays attention when Melody indicates she wants better books.

4. The year is awesome because Melody listens to books, such as the Baby-Sitters Club series, the Goosebumps series, and books by Beverly Cleary. Melody also shows that she comprehends what she is reading.

Making Connections—Section 1: Chapters 1–7 (page 22)

Possible characters include Mrs. V, Melody's parents, Mrs. Tracy, and the classroom aides. Ways of support can include feeding and transporting Melody, communicating with her, recognizing her interests and abilities, etc.

During-Reading Vocabulary Activity—Section 2: Chapters 8–13 (page 26)

1. Penny has a hat **obsession** because she wears a lot of hats, and she puts hats on her stuffed animal and on the dog.

2. Mrs. Lovelace says music can **influence** people by connecting to memories, affecting mood, and affecting responses to problems.

Close Reading the Literature—Section 2: Chapters 8–13 (page 31)

1. There are red-bronze leaves and bright gold sunlight. Melody says it is like leftover summer.

2. Penny loves to dress up, wearing fancy church hats and jewelry—and she's just two years old.

3. Melody says she laughs about Penny's display of attitude.

4. Melody would draw a rose with "a velvety red bloom and a green stem and yellow-green leaves coming from it" for Rose, because she's pretty and delicate and nice to be around.

Making Connections—Section 2: Chapters 8–13 (page 32)

Students should make logical, sound arguments in support of whatever cause they support. The letter should have a heading, salutation, body, closing, and signature.

Close Reading the Literature—Section 3: Chapters 14–20 (page 41)

1. Possible inferences include that the week passes by quickly, Melody is very dedicated to the competition; and the competition preparation is a team effort because Melody is studying with Mrs. V, Dad, Mom, and Catherine.

2. Melody types different answers to the question, "What's wrong with you?" One is polite, and the other is for rude people, such as Claire and Molly. It shows that she's thoughtful, funny, and determined.

3. The setting is calm and quiet. Yet we know from Melody's narration that winter isn't over yet. The setting also provides inspiration for Mrs. V's question to Melody about flying.

4. Mrs. V tells Melody that she will fly when she takes the test, largely because she is so well prepared. Melody also flies because she has the computer to help her show her intelligence. Students may also mention Melody's excellent use of humor as she deals with her limitations.

During-Reading Vocabulary Activity—Section 4: Chapters 21–26 (page 46)

1. Mr. Dimming makes the practices **mandatory** because he wants the team to do very well at the competition.

2. No one wants to mention the **incident** at the restaurant because it was embarrassing for Claire.

Close Reading the Literature—Section 4: Chapters 21–26 (page 51)

1. Mr. Dimming assumes that Connor has a big appetite, and he teases Connor about eating too much.

2. Rose, Elena, and Connor talk about how Melody has been important to the team and did a great job at the competition. She feels as though her balloon has been popped when Molly disagrees with their comments.

3. Melody probably doesn't want to be carried up the stairs because she doesn't want the extra attention it would put on her. She probably feels as though other people will stare and make fun of her.

4. The author brings the reader right into the scene by repeating the effort for each of the five steps: "Pull. Roll up. Bump. First step," and so on.

Close Reading the Literature—Section 5: Chapters 27–33 (page 61)

1. Melody has a lot of the same things to worry about as the other kids, including not knowing if she's cool, having homework, dealing with parents, wanting the "right" clothes, wanting to play and be grown up, having underarm odor, and fitting in.

2. It's difficult to solve a puzzle without some sort of guide. Melody is unsure of what her "picture" will look like because she is not sure she even has all the pieces.

3. Melody probably doesn't mind because she feels badly for Penny.

4. The title could have various interpretations, including but not limited to: Melody feels crazy at times; Melody deals with the world out of her mind because she is limited to her thoughts; or that Melody can only communicate out of her mind through the computer.

Making Connections—Section 5: Chapters 27–33 (page 62)

Answers will vary, although it is expected that the following would receive high marks: Melody, Mrs. V, Catherine, Mom, and Dad. These would receive mediocre to poor grades: Rose, Mr. Dimming, Molly, and Claire.

Comprehension Assessment (pages 67–68)

1. D. capability

2. F. "We were going to be in a *regular* classroom!"

3. Main idea: A computer would let Melody communicate.

4. Supporting Details: F. Melody realizes that Stephen Hawking uses a computer. G. Computers can be adapted for users with special needs.

5. C. Don't let your disability interfere with your ability.

6. E. Melody: "It limits my body, but not my mind."

7. The sentences show Mr. Dimming's discomfort with having to face Melody after the competition.

8. A. "No one seems to know what to say."